CW01332813

OFF

My chest

Breathe. Write. Heal.
A Guided Journal to Self-heal

Also by Hoda Y. E.

Know Yourself:
A Guided Journal for Self-discovery

Know Your Partner:
A Couples' Journey to a Deeper Connection

Be Wiser:
The Enlightenment Path:
A Guided Journal for Wisdom Seekers

Me. The Inner Child:
Reclaiming Wholeness:
A Guided Journal for Healing Your Inner child

Be You:
A Guided Journal for Self-acceptance

***

The Mood
Tracker Journal

The Thought
Tracker Journal

Why do I feel this way?

This journal is for the brave souls ready to journey inward. It's a safe space to dig deep, to explore your emotions, and to embrace your vulnerabilities. Unlock the doors to self-understanding, healing, and a life lived with purpose and authenticity.

With every prompt, question, and blank page, you're given an opportunity to confront your fears, acknowledge your emotions, dismantle the barriers you've built, and discover the wisdom that comes from true self-awareness. Come as you are, start this journey with an open heart, and leave with a clearer sense of who you wish to become.

A journal isn't just a book filled with words — it's a sanctuary where your soul can exhale.

Breathe. Write. Heal

A Guided Journal to Self-heal

OFF

My chest

MUSHIN PRESS

Thoughtful books about deep explorations of inner landscapes, quietly voyaging the self. Published by Mushin Press Cambridgeshire.

Mushin Press

Copyright © 2023 by Hoda Y. E.
All rights reserved.
Cover design by Tata Sekaki.

No part of this book may be reproduced in any form or by any electronic or mechanical means, including information storage and retrieval systems, without written permission from the author, except for the use of brief quotations in a book review.

Contents

Introduction	11
List of emotions	19
Your overthinking mind	25
Just not feeling well	55
Things out of your control	89
Bottled up in your chest	109
No one needs to know	157
Your broken heart	183
Lost & confused	217
Your past	241
Fears of the future	269
Finding you	297
Life	359
Your childhood	399
The road to healing	433
Reflections	532
Free mood journal	537

Introduction

There is a sense of relief when you get things off your chest. When you take a moment to write down every emotion and thought that lifts something 'off your chest', it paves the way to reduce symptoms of anxienty, depression, and trauma.

Words are powerful. Written words even more. That's why paying attention to what we think is so important, and writing those thoughts onto paper is evermore significant. By doing so, we can literally rewire new neuro pathways, writing our own future, rather than letting the brain respond to a negative experience by default.

The idea of digging deeper into our emotions isn't a new one, but it's ever relevant. Our emotions serve as guideposts, signalling what matters to us, what needs to change, and where we might need healing. Ignoring these emotional signals is akin to driving a car with a dashboard full of warning lights — eventually, something, will break down.

Unaddressed emotions have a way of resurfacing, often at inappropriate times or in unhealthy ways.

Suppressed anger can lead to passive-aggressive behaviour, or explosive outbursts. Unresolved fear may manifest as anxiety or phobias. Hidden insecurities could sabotage our relationships. It's only by facing these emotions, by bringing them to the surface and examining them, that we can hope to understand their origins, their meanings, and how best to transform them.

Similarly, stress, more often than we realize, manifests not just in our minds but also in our bodies. When we're constantly on edge, our body releases the hormone cortisol, which historically served as a survival mechanism, prompting fat storage around our abdomen. However, in today's world, this often results in stubborn belly fat, a lingering sign of our internal battles. Journaling offers a sanctuary for our thoughts, a space where we can confront, process, and release these stresses. By pouring our feelings onto paper, we are not just expressing but understanding ourselves better. In doing so, we nurture both our mental well-being and physical health, reminding us that healing often starts from within.

This journal serves as a tool to facilitate that exploration. It aims to be your companion in the challenging but rewarding journey of emotional self-discovery. The questions and prompts within these pages are designed to draw out thoughts, fears, and feelings you might not even know you were harbouring. It's a safe space to confront your innermost struggles and hopes, your darkest fears and most luminous dreams.

As you navigate through the various themes and questions, you might experience discomfort or resistance — that's okay. Self-exploration isn't always easy, but it's essential. You're peeling back layers, shedding old skins, and revealing a more authentic version of yourself, one that's been there all along but may have been obscured by life's constant challenges.

Identifying your precise emotions before journaling is a crucial step on the journey to healing. Pinpointing and naming each emotion provides clarity and a focused direction for self-exploration.

Doing so turns a jumbled, confusing mix of feelings into clear, identifiable emotions, making the process of journaling more straightforward and effective. So, for each question, ask yourself: 'which emotions am I feeling right now?' You'll discover that just the act of identifying and naming your emotions can bring an immediate sense of relief and lightness.

Once you have identified exactly how you feel, take the next empowering step by asking yourself: 'What do I need?' This question shifts the focus from problem to solution, guiding you towards actionable steps that cater to your emotional well-being. Perhaps you need comfort, connection, rest, or simply the space to express yourself. By tuning into your needs, you open up a dialogue with yourself that honors your experiences and begins the process of self-care and healing.

You can choose to keep or tear the page, but write without judging yourself. Let your pen flow as freely as your thoughts. And be honest with yourself and how you truly feel. After all, this is a journey not to some distant shore, but to the centre of who you are — a safe space to unburden and heal your heart.

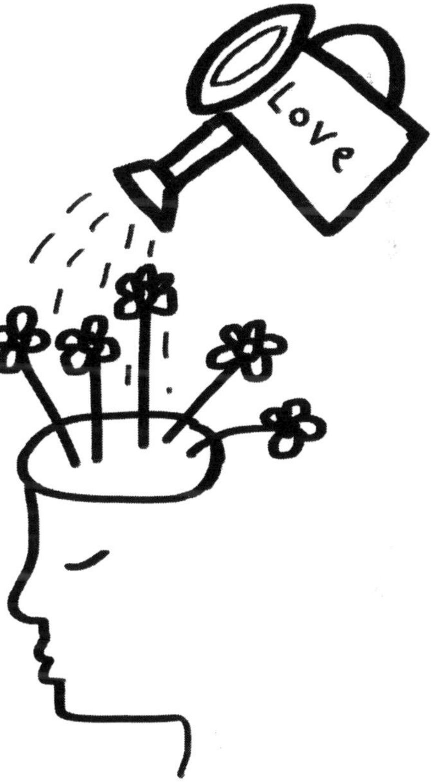
Love

NOTES

1   Pinpoint exactly what you are feeling.

2   Identify what you need.

3   Determine what steps you can take to address your needs.

4   Journal your thoughts.

What are you feeling?

- Agitated
- Alienated
- Angry
- Annoyed
- Anxious
- Apathetic
- Apologetic
- Ashamed
- Belittled
- Betrayed
- Bitter
- Bored
- Burdened
- Clouded
- Confused
- Defeated
- Demoralized
- Demotivated
- Depressed
- Despaired
- Desperate
- Devastated
- Disappointed
- Disgusted
- Disheartened

- Disillusioned
- Distant
- Distressed
- Doubtful
- Drained
- Edgy
- Embarrassed
- Energyless
- Enraged
- Envious
- Exhausted
- Fatigued
- Fearful
- Fed up
- Flustered
- Frightened
- Frustrated
- Guilty
- Heartbroken
- Helpless
- Hesitant
- Hopeless
- Humiliated
- Hurt
- Impatient

- Inadequate
- Insecure
- Intimidated
- Irritated
- Isolated
- Jealous
- Lonely
- Lost
- Misunderstood
- Moody
- Mournful
- Neglected
- Nervous
- Offended
- Outraged
- Overburdened
- Overwhelmed
- Panicky
- Pessimistic
- Powerless
- Pressured
- Regretful
- Rejected
- Remorseful
- Resentful

- Restless
- Sad
- Self-loathing
- Scared
- Shaken
- Sorrowful
- Sorry
- Speechless
- Stressed
- Tired
- Tormented
- Traumatised
- Troubled
- Uncertain
- Uneasy
- Unhappy
- Unsettled
- Unstable
- Unworthy
- Upset
- Vulnerable
- Weary
- Withdrawn
- Worried
- Wretched

What do you need?

- Acceptance
- Adventure
- Affection
- Appreciation
- Autonomy
- Alone time
- Belonging
- Boundaries
- Care
- Change
- Clarity
- Closure
- Comfort
- Community
- Compassion
- Declutter
- Discipline
- Emotional release
- Emotional safety
- Empathy
- Empowerment
- Energy
- Equality
- Exercise
- Freedom
- Fresh air
- Friendship
- Fun and play
- Goal setting
- God
- Gratitude
- Guidance
- Growth
- Harmony
- Healing
- Health
- Honesty
- Hug
- Independence
- Innovation
- Insight
- Inspiration
- Integrity
- Intimacy
- Joy and laughter
- Justice
- Knowledge
- Kill routine
- Love
- Meaning
- Mental clarity
- Mindfulness

- Nature
- Nurturance
- Nutrition
- Order
- Patience
- Peace
- Personal space
- Physical health
- Physical safety
- Privacy
- Progress
- Purpose
- Reassurance
- Reflection
- Relaxation
- Respect
- Rest
- Routine
- Romance
- Safety
- Security
- Self-acceptance
- Self-awareness
- Self-care
- Self-compassion
- Self-confidence
- Self-esteem
- Self-expression
- Self-love
- Self-respect
- Self-sufficiency
- Self-validation
- Silence
- Simplicity
- Sleep
- Slow Down
- Social Life
- Space
- Spirituality
- Stability
- Support
- Time
- To be heard
- To let go
- Tranquility
- Transparency
- Trust
- Truth
- Understanding
- Validation
- Variety
- Wisdom

I CAN~~'T~~ HEAL MYSELF

There's a sense of relief when you get things off your chest.

Free your overthinking mind

Overthinking dims the mind's light; clear the fog and set your thoughts free.

Set a timer for 5 minutes and write any thoughts freely that come across your mind. Write as freely as you can. It doesn't have to make sense, but the most important thing is to write without stopping:

The practice of free writing for a set period is like a mental detox, helping you to unload conscious and subconscious thoughts without the interruption of self-censorship or judgment. It's a way of making tangible the swirling thoughts that occupy your mind. Doing this practice helps you understand your mental state at a given moment and can offer insights into your deeper concerns, joys, or preoccupations.

Make a list of your main dominant thoughts today:

Your thoughts shape your reality. Identifying your dominant thoughts allows you to be the architect of your own mindset, consciously choosing which cognitive structures to uphold and which to dismantle. Through this exercise, you gain invaluable insights into themes that currently dominate your life, opening the door for intentional change.

Overthinking

Writing or talking to someone

What things have you come across on social media and how did that make you feel?

Social media can be a landscape of both inspiration and despair, often within the span of a few scrolls. Encountering something that evokes strong emotions is like stumbling upon a landmark in your digital journey — a sign that you're deeply connected to or triggered by certain narratives. Take a step back to ask what these emotions reveal about your beliefs, your desires, and even your insecurities. This self-awareness can become your compass, helping you steer your digital life more consciously.

What things keep you awake at night?

The things that haunt you in the stillness of the night are often echoes of unresolved dilemmas or unspoken desires. Rather than treating them as insomniac enemies, engage with them as nocturnal mentors. They appear in the quiet to invite you to confront what you might evade in the noise of daylight. Listening to them can not only grant you peace but also reveal the contours of your inner landscape, helping you navigate life's complexities with greater ease.

What things do you tend to overthink about and why?

Overthinking is often a symptom of a deeper emotional imbalance, perhaps a need for control, a fear of uncertainty, or an avoidance of painful feelings. It's your mind trying to solve an emotional puzzle. Recognising that overthinking rarely brings clarity but often amplifies confusion can be liberating. The path away from overthinking leads through the heart — by addressing the underlying emotional triggers, you can find the peace that has eluded your racing mind.

List the toxic things you wish to eliminate
in your life:

Toxic elements in our lives serve as both anchors and illusions; they weigh us down but also masquerade as something we need. The act of identifying these toxic elements is like turning on a light in a dark room, revealing the corners where negativity hides. As you shed light on them, you're taking the first, empowering step in a journey that leads to liberation, healing, and transformation.

Just not feeling well

It's okay to admit that today, unlike others, you're just not feeling well.

Write down anything that's bothering you today?

The things that bother us are often reflections of unresolved issues within us. They act as mirrors, revealing not just the external circumstances that irritate us, but also the internal landscapes that we've yet to navigate. Recognizing this can be our first step towards understanding and healing. With every recognition, we inch closer to finding our inner balance and peace.

If someone was a listening ear right now,
what would you express?

The things you wish to say when you have an attentive audience often point to what's most pressing in your life. Verbalising or writing down these thoughts can offer a release and may lead you to proactive solutions. By giving voice to these internal narratives, you initiate a journey from introspection to action, translating inner dialogues into steps towards clarity and resolution.

What things make you sad and bring tear to your eyes and why?

Tears are your soul's way of cleansing emotional dust from the corners of your inner world. While the stimuli that provoke tears can vary, their appearance is always an invitation to pause and examine what matters deeply to you. This moment of vulnerability is also a moment of profound honesty, revealing the soft spots in your emotional armour and pointing you toward what needs healing or understanding.

If no one can hear you screaming, what kind of things would you scream out right now?

The things you'd scream in isolation are likely your rawest, most primal feelings, the ones you might even be hiding from yourself. Acknowledging them can be the first step toward releasing repressed emotions and moving toward genuine peace. By confronting these hidden feelings, you pave a path for healing and self-understanding. It's in this acceptance that transformation begins.

What emotions are you experiencing right now?

Emotions are the language of the soul, often speaking in riddles and metaphors. While we may not always understand them in the moment, each emotion serves as a signpost on the journey of self-discovery, pointing us toward truths we might otherwise overlook.

Who is to blame?

Blame is a web where the paths of pain and accountability intersect, leading us often in circles of unresolved emotion. While it may feel satisfying to assign blame, doing so can also trap you in a cycle of negativity. Instead, focusing on understanding the 'why' behind the 'who' can offer not just closure, but a lesson in empathy, personal responsibility, and growth.

What things stress you out?

Stressors are like psychological allergens, triggering reactions that can affect your well-being. Identifying these stress factors is akin to recognising what substances you're allergic to; it allows you to either avoid them or find effective ways to manage the reactions that they provoke. Understanding your stressors gives you control, empowering you to navigate life's challenges with a bit more ease.

Write down all the things that you feel feed your energy, and the things that steal your energy:

Life is a constant exchange of energy. Recognising what fuels you and what drains you can serve as a personal guidebook for maintaining your vitality. When you consciously make space for what nourishes you and set boundaries against energy thieves, you curate a life that is more aligned with your well-being.

Things out of your control

The art of living isn't about controlling every detail but embracing what's out of your hands.

What things are not within your control?

We often spend energy fretting over events and outcomes we have no power over. Recognising what's beyond our control is the first step toward inner peace and constructive focus. Take a moment to release these burdens; you were never meant to carry them. Emotions that arise from uncontrollable circumstances are like waves in the ocean — temporary and ever-changing. It's okay to feel overwhelmed, anxious, or frustrated. By identifying these emotions, you give yourself permission to process them and eventually let them go.

Can you control or change the situation?

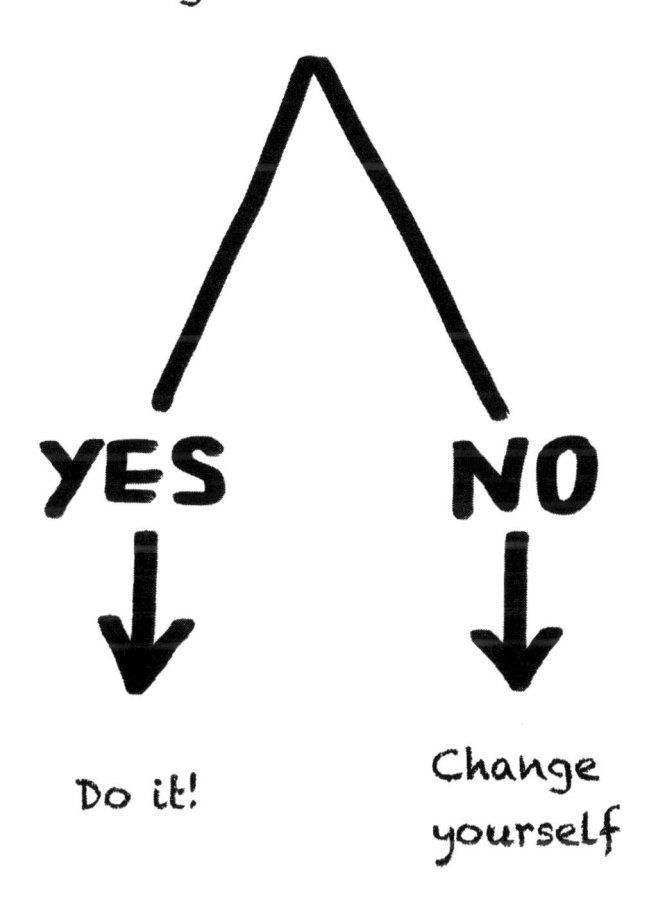

YES → Do it!

NO → Change yourself

What things do you wish to change?

The desire for change is a yearning for evolution. It's your soul's way of nudging you closer to your ideal self. It's crucial to distinguish between what you want to change due to external pressures and what genuinely resonates with your innermost desires. This discernment is the first step in a transformative journey, one that leads not just to change but to a journey of growth.

What things disappoint you?

Disappointment, though a bitter pill, often carries with it a silver-lining of redirection. Consider it life's gentle nudge, ensuring you're on a trajectory that resonates with your truest self. Instead of perceiving it as a setback, embrace disappointment as a valuable teacher. It offers a chance to pause, reflect, and pivot, guiding you closer to paths that will illuminate your purpose and potential. In its essence, disappointment is less about deterring and more about refining your journey to its most authentic and fulfilling course.

Have you had any failures and setbacks?
How did you handle them?

Setbacks and failures are inevitable chapters in the human experience, but they're often the pages where the most growth happens. Reflecting on these instances provides a well-rounded perspective of your resilience, coping strategies, and your ability to adapt and learn. This reflection can be a rich source of insights for future challenges and a testament to your ability to survive and thrive.

Bottled up in your chest

What's bottled up in your chest weighs more than the world on your shoulders. Find freedom and release it.

What have you kept bottled inside for so long?

Bottling emotions is like storing water in a dam; it might serve a purpose for a while, but eventually, the pressure will seek an outlet, often bursting forth in unpredictable ways. These suppressed feelings are part of you, crying out for acknowledgment and expression. Letting them out is not a sign of weakness but a liberating release that can foster deeper self-understanding and emotional equilibrium. Like opening the windows in a musty room, airing out your internal world can bring fresh perspectives.

What was the most painful thing you've ever experienced that wasn't physical?

Emotional or psychological pain, unlike its physical counterpart, leaves scars that are invisible but deeply felt. They can linger for years, a silent testimony to past traumas. Recognizing and confronting these intimate, non-physical wounds is a crucial initial stride towards healing. It paves the way for deep reflection, comprehension, and ultimately, resolution. This journey, although challenging, is essential for unveiling and healing hidden wounds. As pain and emotions surface, they transform into stepping stones of growth.

Do you feel lonely? Why?

Loneliness is not merely a state of solitude; it's an emotional echo chamber amplifying your deepest needs for connection and recognition. It's an invitation to look inward and ask: 'What am I truly missing?' Sometimes, the person you most need to reconnect with is yourself. Reconnecting can turn your loneliness into a fertile ground for self-discovery, allowing you to cultivate more meaningful relationships with others, and a more fulfilling relationship with yourself.

What traumas have you been through?

Traumas are emotional scars, often buried deep, yet eternally part of our emotional DNA. By acknowledging them, you're not giving them power over you but reclaiming your narrative. They are chapters in your life book that you didn't write but must read, not to relive the pain but to understand its place in your larger story. Traumas, if understood, can be teachers, cruel yet enlightening, urging you towards resilience and self-compassion.

Deep down inside what do you want to say?

Sometimes our most authentic feelings and thoughts get buried under social norms, fears, or the simple rush of daily life. Acknowledging what you want to say deep down can be an emancipating act, a reclaiming of your own voice. Even if these words never leave the sanctuary of your own mind or diary, the mere act of formulating them brings clarity and could serve as a first step to meaningful actions.

Are you holding onto any grudge or resentment?

Grudges can be burdensome, their heavy presence lingering in the mind, sapping energy and joy, and obscuring the pathways to forgiveness and inner peace. An invisible luggage that you carry around, weighing you down emotionally and spiritually. Acknowledging these can be akin to setting down that heavy bag and examining its contents. Whether it leads you to a decision to forgive, confront, or simply accept and move on, identifying your grudges is the first step to emotional freedom.

What are your deepest insecurities and how can you turn them into strengths?

When you examine your deepest insecurities, understand that they are like internal fault lines shaped by various emotional and experiential tectonics over the years. Rather than perceiving them as permanent weaknesses, consider them areas awaiting your love, attention, and improvement. Acknowledging your insecurities can be a vulnerable yet liberating experience, the first step toward mastering them. Your awareness makes them lose their power, and bit by bit, you reclaim your self-assurance, recognising that these insecurities are not your identity but rather challenges to be met and transcended.

What things hurt you?

Recognising what causes you emotional pain is not an admission of weakness but a stride toward self-awareness. Emotional pain, while unpleasant, serves as a compass pointing towards the aspects of life that require your attention and healing. Understanding your emotional triggers enables you to build a mental and emotional toolkit for resilience and growth.

What things make you jealous or angry?

Jealousy and anger, rather than mere emotional outbursts, are your inner compass pointing towards unresolved issues or unmet needs. They emerge not to torment, but to teach. Instead of seeing them as adversaries, regard them as mentors that reveal the deepest corners of your psyche. By understanding their origins and embracing their lessons, you can transform these emotions from disruptive forces into catalysts for personal growth and self-awareness.

I feel ~~Annoyed~~ ~~Irritated~~ ~~Frustrated~~ ANGRY!

It's healthy to pinpoint and validate your exact feelings.

Has anyone around you let you down?

When someone lets you down, it can feel like a breach in the very contract of your relationship with them. It's crucial to remember that people are complex creatures, navigating their own struggles, fears, and shortcomings. Their actions toward you are often more a reflection of their own internal landscape than a commentary on your worth. While you can't control their actions, you can control your reaction. This is where your power lies, in choosing to respond in a way that aligns with your values and contributes to your own well-being.

Connect to God, write down a prayer:

In prayer, we find a sacred dialogue, a direct line to the Divine. The act of writing down your prayers imbues them with a sense of tangible reality, converting abstract pleas into concrete affirmations. Whether you're seeking guidance, giving thanks, or simply looking for solace, the ink on the paper is a beautiful way to connect to God.

No one needs to know

To make your heart lighter, whisper to the wind the secrets no one needs to know.

List the secrets you wish no one to know?

Holding onto secrets can feel like carrying heavy stones in your pockets as you wade through the river of life — each one slows you down a bit more, making every step more burdensome. Recognise that your secrets, though concealed from the world, are fully visible to your own self, and the act of hiding them often consumes more energy than confronting them. The fear of being 'found out' can haunt you, but remember that everyone has their own stones to carry; acknowledging yours could be the first step in lightening your load and making room for more meaningful pursuits.

What things are you ashamed of?

The things we are ashamed of often sit like shadows in the backdrop of our consciousness, subtly influencing our actions, decisions, and self-esteem. Shame is a cloak woven from threads of past mistakes, societal judgments, and personal fears; yet, it's a garment we are not bound to wear forever. Acknowledging your shame is akin to standing in front of a mirror and truly seeing yourself, flaws and all, realizing that imperfection is not inadequacy. Shedding light on what you're ashamed of often dissipates its power, freeing you to wear a new cloak, one of self-acceptance.

What are your deepest fears?

Fear is a labyrinthine cave that holds not just monsters but also hidden treasures. While it confines you, it also offers clues to your deepest vulnerabilities and untapped potentials. Embrace your fears as reluctant messengers that, when listened to and undestood, can illuminate the path toward courage, resilience, and a fuller experience of life. Understanding fear is a lantern lighting up another dark corner of your internal world.

What is it that you want to say to that someone, yet haven't found the courage to say?

Unspoken words can become burdens, heavy loads carried silently. Identifying these suppressed sentiments can be the precursor to either finding the courage to express them or realising the reasons for your hesitance. Either way, it's a step toward emotional freedom.

Is there anything that you are not proud of?

Owning up to your own flaws or past mistakes isn't easy, but it's crucial for growth and self-awareness. Moments of shame or regret can hang around in your emotional background, subtly influencing your decisions and self-esteem. Fully acknowledging these can be both painful and liberating, but it's the first step towards accountability, making amends, or internal change.

What things would you like to tell someone if this was the last day of your life?

The urgency of a hypothetical 'last day' strips away the masks we wear and the fears that keep us silent. It propels you to voice the unspoken love, gratitude, or even grievances that you carry within you. These are the things that matter. Realising this can be a profound revelation; why wait for a last day that may never come? Seize the day to express your truths, for in doing so, you bring your inner world into alignment with your outer life.

Your broken heart

In the healing process of a broken heart, we often find paths we never knew existed.

Who broke your heart? And what small steps can you take to feel whole again?

Life is the most relentless yet insightful teacher. Every experience, good or bad, comes with its set of lessons. Taking stock of what you've learned so far is like flipping through a personal textbook of wisdom. These lessons often serve as guiding principles, shaping your decisions, your reactions, and your values. A broken heart, though it may feel like the cruelest of these lessons, imparts a depth of understanding and compassion like no other. It is in the quiet moments of reflection that one realizes, while the heart might have been shattered, it is piecing itself back together, stronger and more resilient than before.

What do you want the person you love the most to say to you?

The words we wish to hear from loved ones often reflect our deepest needs and desires, be it validation, affection, or to simply be understood. Identifying these desired can be enlightening, exposing not just what you seek from others but what you may need to give yourself.

Write a letter to all those who have hurt you in your life:

Writing a letter to those who have hurt you is like opening a pressure valve on a well of stored emotions. This isn't about them, it's about you, your healing, and your journey. The paper can hold your anger, your sorrow, and your forgiveness, allowing you to clear emotional space for peace, understanding, and future happiness. Whether or not you send it, the mere act of writing it is a step toward liberation.

What things make you sad?

The things that bring us sorrow often serve as mirrors reflecting unmet needs or desires, be they emotional, social, or personal. Identifying what makes you sad is like shining a light in the dark corners of your inner world, illuminating areas that may require attention or healing.

How do you wish to be loved?

Your 'love language' is a direct reflection of your deepest emotional needs. Identifying how you wish to be loved can not only improve your relationships but also your self-love practices. This recognition illuminates the pathways to fulfillment in interpersonal dynamics and underscores the means to nourishing self-affection, bridging the space between external connections and internal harmony.

Where do you wish to be and with whom right at this given moment if nothing can stop you?

Fantasies of where you'd rather be and with whom are more than mere escapism; they are windows into your soul's longing. These unfiltered desires can serve as a compass, pointing towards what truly matters to you and perhaps what's missing in your current reality.

What heartbreaks have you been through?

Heartbreaks are very much like emotional earthquakes, shaking your world to its core, yet also redesigning your emotional landscape. They're painful, yes, but also profound experiences, carving out spaces in your heart for deeper understanding, empathy, and eventually, renewed love. Each heartbreak comes with its own lesson in vulnerability and strength, teaching you how precious it is to love and be loved, even if that love was not meant to last.

When was the last time you had an open honest conversation with someone? If you had the opportunity to have one, what would you say?

Open, honest conversations serve as emotional outlets, opportunities for intellectual growth, and sometimes even therapy. The frequency, or lack thereof, of such exchanges in your life may point to your emotional openness or vulnerabilities. Should the chance for such a conversation arise right now, what you'd choose to say would likely highlight your most pressing concerns, dreams, or emotional needs.

Lost & Confused

Every person, at some point, feels lost and adrift. Even the wisest pause for moments of reflection, using them as a chance to realign with their true path.

What is your purpose in life?

The question of life's purpose is as old as humanity itself, and often leads to existential exploration. In the midst of this vast quest, the practices of meditation, reflection, and taking intentional pauses can serve as powerful tools. These moments of stillness allow us to tune into our inner voices, drowned out by the noise of daily life.

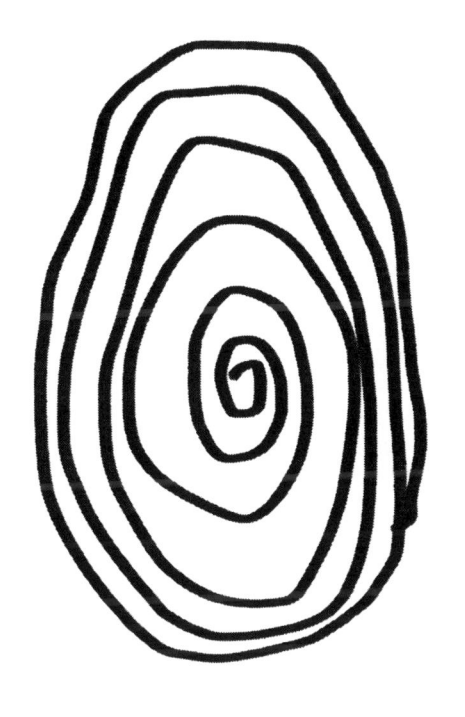

Only you hold your fingerprints as a reminder that your imprint in this world is unique.

Write about a time when you faced a major life crossroad:

Life's crossroads are not just decisions, they're narrative forks, each path leading to a different version of yourself. Whether you took the road less travelled or followed the crowd, your choice became a cornerstone in the architecture of your life story. Revisiting that decision can offer insights into your values, your courage, and even your fears, teaching you more about who you were, who you are, and who you're becoming.

Write about a time when you faced a difficult decision:

Difficult decisions are defining moments that often alter the course of your life. Reflecting on how you navigated such crossroads can provide invaluable insights into your decision-making process, personal values, and the outcomes that followed.

What unresolved conflicts do you need to address?

Unresolved conflicts are emotional time bombs silently ticking away, amassing stress and unease in their wake. By identifying these conflicts, you're halfway towards defusing them. Whether it's a fallout with a loved one or an internal strife related to choices and identities, acknowledging them provides an opening for constructive conversations and self-reflection, potentially leading to reconciliation or at least, clarity.

If this was your last day, what legacy would you like to leave?

The legacy you wish to leave behind speaks volumes about the person you are and the values you hold dear. It's a mirror reflecting your most cherished relationships and your most impactful deeds. Imagining how others would remember you can be a sobering exercise in evaluating your life's current trajectory and considering whether it aligns with your deeper, long-lasting objectives.

Your past

Our scars are not reminders of pain, but testaments to resilience and the journey of healing.

Is there a memory you want to block out and why?

The desire to block out a memory is a protective instinct, a mental armour your mind adopts to shield you from emotional wounds. Yet, repressed memories are like stones in the river of your consciousness; they may disappear beneath the surface but their presence changes the flow of your thoughts and feelings. Confronting these memories is the first step in removing the stones that obstruct your emotional river, allowing you to flow more freely toward healing and wholeness.

If you can turn back time, what would you do differently and why?

Regret is a challenging emotion that often comes with a lesson attached. Identifying your 'do overs' not only helps you confront these lessons but can guide your actions in the present and future. In unraveling these threads of the past, we carve pathways of wisdom and growth, transforming past missteps into stepping stones for enlightened decision-making and enriched self-understanding.

What are the worst moments or days in your life?

As you reflect upon the worst moments of your life, remember that these periods, however dark, are integral chapters in the story of your becoming. These trials test not just your resilience but also your humanity, pushing you to find light in the darkest corridors of your existence. While it's challenging to find the silver-lining when you're in the eye of the storm, remember that storms also bring rain to barren lands; they contribute to new growth, teaching you invaluable lessons in endurance and renewal that you wouldn't learn any other way.

Take 10 deep breaths and with each breath inhale the future, exhale the past. Journal your feelings and thoughts:

Breathing is the rhythm of life, each inhale and exhale is a moment of pure existence. When you intentionally breathe in the future and breathe out the past, you're harmonising with the eternal now. This simple act can become a powerful ritual, aligning your emotional and mental state with a sense of limitless potential and a release of what no longer serves you. Journaling these feelings translates this ephemeral experience into a tangible form, solidifying its transformative power.

> We suffer more in imagination than in reality

Is there anything in your past you wish to write about?

Our pasts are treasure troves of experiences, filled with lessons, emotions, and turning points. Writing about them isn't an act of dwelling in bygones but an opportunity to reflect and perhaps reframe. By putting words to your history, you give it shape and meaning, offering yourself a chance to understand how those past moments contribute to who you are today.

List the things you forgive yourself for:

Forgiving ourselves is akin to planting a seed in a garden that has been ravaged by winter. The landscape of your soul may be littered with frosty memories and actions you regret, but forgiveness brings the spring of renewal. It nurtures the soil of your conscience, allowing new buds of self-love and compassion to sprout. In forgiving yourself, you aren't erasing past errors but enriching your inner world to grow different outcomes in the future. It's the commitment to nourish your own well-being, unburdened by the weight of internal judgments.

Fears of the future

Our fears of the future stem from the unknown, but with preparation and courage, we can illuminate our path.

What worries do you have about the future?

Worries about the future are like dark clouds on your mental horizon, subtle yet persistent reminders of uncertainties and risks. While you cannot control what the future holds, understanding your specific worries can help you prepare and perhaps find a semblance of peace in the present. In acknowledging these anxieties, you grant yourself the power to mitigate their impact, fostering resilience and equipping yourself with strategies to course potential challenges with grace.

Do you fear death and what does death mean to you?

Death often looms like a distant shadow, an inevitable end that many prefer not to dwell upon. To understand death is not just to grapple with the end, but to engage with the profound questions of what it means to live. This understanding can act as a compass, guiding how you navigate life's journey — it can inspire you to live with intention, to forge genuine connections, and to find purpose and truth in life.

Write a letter to your future self, describing where you hope to be:

This exercise is a promise to your future self, a time capsule of aspirations and a yardstick for future reflection. It encapsulates not just your dreams, but also serves as a motivational guidebook. As you pen down your hopes and dreams, you're committing to them in a tangible form, making them more real and consequently, more attainable. When you eventually read this letter in the future, it will serve as a poignant reminder of who you were and how far you've come — or what still needs attention.

How do you handle change? And how do you adapt to new circumstances?

Change is the only constant, yet our adaptability to it varies immensely. Your comfort or struggle with change can reveal much about your emotional resilience, flexibility, and your underlying fears or expectations. Whether you view change as an adventure or a challenge speaks to your worldview and can inform how you navigate the inevitable shifts that life will bring.

Overthinking
& worrying

Not resisting
what is

List any thoughts that cross your mind about the future:

Our minds are veritable time machines, ceaselessly oscillating between the nostalgia of the past and the anticipations of the future. Taking stock of these thoughts can be like reading the journal of your subconscious, laying bare your inner preoccupations, regrets, and hopes. By making a conscious effort to list them, you create an emotional inventory that could serve as a map, guiding you to the issues that need your attention, or the dreams that are begging to be realised.

If today was the last day of your life,
what kind of things would you do?

This morbid yet powerful thought experiment forces you to distill life down to its essence. It helps you prioritise what truly matters, revealing where you might want to direct your energy and attention in the limited time we all have.

Finding you

Every path you take, every challenge you face, is a step closer to finding yourself.

What do you really think about yourself?

Your self-perception is the lens through which you experience the world. While it might be tinted with societal expectations or past experiences, this lens is not fixed; it can be adjusted, cleaned, or even replaced. Taking time to really think about how you see yourself opens the door to self-improvement, self-acceptance, and most importantly self-love, aligning your inner view with the reality of who you are and who you wish to be.

Who are you and who do you want to be? - What small steps can you take to make that happen?

You are not a fixed point but a flowing river, ever-changing and evergrowing. The 'you' that you wish to become should not be a restrictive mold but a liberating possibility, a journey of becoming more authentically yourself. The space between who you are and who you want to be is not a chasm of inadequacy, but a bridge built on the pillars of growth and self-exploration.

Are you proud of who you are?

To be proud of who you are means to stand tall in your own truth, unswayed by societal judgments or external validation. It's a form of internal integrity that allows you to look in the mirror and acknowledge not just your achievements, but also your struggles and imperfections — viewing them not as flaws, but valuable chapters in your unique story. When you embrace your authentic self, flaws and all, you give permission for your soul to breathe freely, unencumbered by the weight of expectations or self-doubt.

Why do you have to be perfect?

The pursuit of perfection can be a double-edged sword. On one hand, it drives you to improve, but on the other, it can become a source of endless stress and feelings of inadequacy. Digging deep to understand why you feel compelled to reach an often unattainable standard can reveal underlying insecurities, societal pressures, or even past experiences that have shaped this mindset. Once identified, you can work towards a more forgiving, balanced view of yourself.

What's your favourite ways to express yourself?

Expression is your personal signature on the world, a declaration of your unique existence. Understanding your preferred modes of expression can enrich your experience of life, allowing you to communicate and connect in ways that bring you joy, validation, and a sense of purpose.

Do you love yourself?

Self-love isn't a destination but a journey; it's the daily practice of granting yourself the same compassion and understanding that you offer to others. As you learn to love yourself more, you pave the way for love, light, and healing to enter your life.

What things would you change about yourself and why?

The desire for self-improvement is both human and universal. However, the reasons behind these desired changes often reveal deeper layers of your self-perception and values. Articulating these reasons can help you distinguish between changes that are superficially imposed by societal norms and those that will lead to genuine growth.

What are your core values and beliefs? And are you living in alignment with your values and beliefs?

Your core values and beliefs are the backbone of your identity. Assessing whether your life aligns with these principles is a measure of your own integrity. Misalignment often leads to a sense of disarray or dissatisfaction, signalling the need for recalibration. When such disarray surfaces, it acts as an alert, a call to re-evaluate. It's an opportunity to pause and reflect, to peer into the depths of one's soul and question the paths we are treading.

What are your weaknesses? What baby steps can you take to change your weaknesses into strengths?

Admitting your weaknesses is not a confession of failure but an acknowledgment of your humanity. Each weakness marks an area of potential growth, a chink in your armour that you can either choose to fortify or accept as part of your unique make up. By being honest about your vulnerabilities, you create opportunities for improvement, greater self-awareness, and more authentic connections with others.

Who do you constantly compare yourself to and why?

The act of constant comparison is like trying to measure the ocean's depth with a ruler; it's both futile and exhausting. Each person's journey is as unique as their fingerprint, marked by a specific set of opportunities, challenges, and timelines. When you catch yourself comparing, understand that it often stems from a void of insecurity or a lack of self-affirmation. Work on filling that void not with external validations but with self-generated metrics of success and happiness. Your life's worth can't be determined by a side by side assessment with someone else; it's a delicate web that only you can solve.

When and where do you mostly feel like you are you?

This question is an exploration of authenticity and belonging. The environments and circumstances where you most feel like 'you' are likely where you feel most free, loved, or engaged. These are the spaces and moments where your mask comes off and your soul feels at home. Understanding where this happens can guide you in choosing life situations, relationships, and careers that allow your true self to flourish.

Do you ever feel inferior or less important?
If so, when, where and with who?

Feelings of inferiority are more than emotional states; they are windows into the corners of our psyche where self-doubt and insecurities dwell. Identifying when and with whom these feelings arise can provide actionable insights into your own self-esteem and guide you toward relationships and environments that uplift rather than undermine.

Write down how you think the world perceives you and how you wish to be perceived:

The perception gap between how the world sees you and how you wish to be seen can be both enlightening and disheartening. But in that gap lies an opportunity for growth and self-discovery. It's not about changing yourself to fit external expectations but rather adjusting the lens through which you project yourself, so it aligns more closely with your true essence.

Do you have any dreams that you've since forgotten or abandoned? - Why?

Forgotten dreams are like stars obscured by the light pollution of daily responsibilities and self-doubt. They may fade but they're never truly gone. Revisiting these dreams isn't an exercise in nostalgia, but an act of rediscovery. It's an invitation to remember the passions that once fueled you and consider how they might be reincorporated into your life. Even if the form of your dreams changes, their essence can still guide you.

Write a letter to your younger self — what would you say?

A letter to your younger self is a conversation across time, offering wisdom in hindsight to the person you once were. This act is inherently one of kindness, a way to gently hold your past naivety or errors in judgment and say, 'It's okay; you did your best with what you knew'. This dialogue with your younger self also allows you to crystallise the lessons you've gathered along the way, making them touchstones for your ongoing journey.

Life

Life's surprises are like unwrapped gifts; they may not always be what we want, but they often contain what we need.

How has life disappointed you?

Disappointment is not a dead end, but a detour sign pointing toward unseen vistas of possibility. As you navigate the winding roads of life, allow your disappointments to guide you, leading you to a destination richer in experience and wisdom than you had originally planned.

What things are you resisting right now?

Resistance is often an emotional wall we build to protect ourselves. Identifying what you are resisting may help you understand what it is you're truly afraid of facing. Doing so could be the first step in tearing down that wall. In dismantling these barriers, we embark on a journey of vulnerability and strength, where facing our fears becomes a conduit for transformative growth.

Resisting what is

Accepting what is

What are your deepest struggles in life?

Acknowledging deep struggles is like laying the groundwork for your own epic story. These are the conflicts that shape you, test you, and ultimately contribute to your personal growth. By identifying them, you can also map out a path to resolve those struggles. Every challenge faced becomes a chapter of victory, each resolution, a testament to your resilience and strength.

Are you content with yourself and life?

Contentment is a nuanced emotion that intertwines with your perception of success, aspirations, and daily experiences. Being content doesn't mean you lack ambition or goals; rather, it suggests a form of emotional equilibrium, a baseline happiness that persists despite life's ups and downs. If you find it difficult to answer this question, it may highlight areas in your life that are sources of unrest or discontent.

What are your life regrets and why?

Regrets are timelines of 'what could have been', but they are also teachers in the school of hard knocks. While you may wish to turn back the hands of time, the fact remains that regrets also offer valuable life lessons. Acknowledging them without self-judgment can be an act of courageous self-honesty, transforming regret from a burden into a stepping stone toward a wiser and stronger you.

In what way do you wish for people to accept you?

The desire for acceptance is fundamentally a quest for safety and love. Detailing the specific forms of acceptance you seek provides a blueprint for meaningful relationships and self-validation. In this exploration, connections are deepened and the journey of self-discovery is enriched, fostering a harmonious balance between the love we seek externally and the love we nurture within ourselves.

Are you living a life that's true to yourself,
or are you trying to please others?

This introspective question beckons you to take stock of your authenticity. Are your choices genuinely yours or are they unduly influenced by expectations, societal norms, or loved ones? Each scenario has its own set of consequences: a life true to yourself brings inner peace but may involve difficult choices, while a life aimed at pleasing others might offer external validation but may come with the cost of your own happiness or self-respect.

What do you hate about your life and what small steps can you take to make changes?

Hate is a strong emotion, but when directed towards aspects of your own life, it acts as a glaring signpost pointing toward deep-rooted dissatisfaction or unmet needs. This harsh self-assessment could be a springboard for change, prompting you to take drastic measures to alter the conditions that provoke such strong negativity. It also begs for introspection: understanding why you feel this way could unearth issues that may require not just situational changes but also emotional or psychological healing.

How can you simplify your life and reduce stress?

Simplifying life is about returning to the essentials, paring down the noise, obligations, and complexities that stress you out. It could mean decluttering your physical space, setting boundaries in relationships, or prioritising your well-being. The act of simplifying often leads to a clearer mind, better emotional health, and a more focused life.

Your childhood

The pains of a bitter childhood can either tether one's spirit or give wings to newfound strength.

List some of your sad childhood memories:

Revisiting sad childhood memories is like walking through an old, dusty attic. It's a somber journey, but each memory is a relic of your past that has contributed to your present self. Acknowledging these moments, without dwelling on them, so can provide a clearer understanding of how your past has shaped your present and what emotional wounds may need attention.

Can you recall any challenging or traumatic experiences from your childhood?

Childhood traumas act like deep imprints on the soft clay of your developing self. They shape not just your memories but your perceptions and reactions to the world. Yet, remember that clay can be remoulded. While past traumas may have shaped you, they don't have to define you. Acknowledging these experiences is the first step in reclaiming your narrative and sculpting a future where you're not a victim, but a survivor who has the power to define your own destiny.

Do you feel your parents or caregivers loved you enough as a child?

The perception of parental love often shapes our self-worth and expectations in relationships. Reflecting on this can be a way to understand some of your deepest emotional patterns, and perhaps heal old wounds.

Do you blame your parents or caregivers for anything in your childhood?

Parental influence is often deeply complex, woven from threads of love, neglect, encouragement, and criticism. While it's natural to blame our parents or caregivers for certain aspects of our upbringing, taking time to evaluate these feelings can lead to powerful realisations. Understanding that they, too, make mistakes and are products of their own circumstances can be the first step toward healing and forging a new relationship with them, based on adult perspectives rather than childlike dependencies.

Do you ever feel that you let your parents or caregivers down in any way?

The feeling of letting your parents or caregivers down often springs from a well of unrealized expectations — either theirs or your own. Remember, your life is not a theater performance played to a script they've written. It's your unique journey, and sometimes the roads you need to take might not align with theirs. Granting yourself the permission to be imperfectly you is the first step in liberating yourself from the shackles of undue expectations and the commencement of writing your own life story.

What expectations from your parents, caregivers or loved ones do you want?

Expectations from our loved ones often form the unseen emotional contracts that govern our relationships. If these expectations are unmet or unspoken, they can lead to feelings of disappointment or dissatisfaction. Identifying and acknowledging what you yearn for from your parents or loved ones not only provides clarity but also offers an opportunity to improve the quality of these important relationships.

Where you ever bullied as a child? How did those experiences shape who you are today?

Childhood bullying is a storm that leaves lasting impressions on the landscape of your self-esteem. The experience, while scarring, often molds you into a person of empathy and resilience. It teaches the painful yet vital lessons about human nature, vulnerability, and the importance of kindness. Recognising how this has shaped you can turn a negative history into a platform for advocacy, self-improvement, or even just a deeper understanding of others' struggles.

What life lessons have you learned from your parents or caregivers?

The fabric of your upbringing is woven with life lessons, some appear explicit, others gleaned from observation. These formative teachings, whether beneficial or cautionary, shape your worldview, your ethics, and your strategies for navigating life. Identifying these lessons can give you insight into your own beliefs and values.

The road to healing

On the journey of recovery, every step, no matter how small, moves us closer to tranquility. Each day on the healing journey brings its own challenges, but also its own rewards.

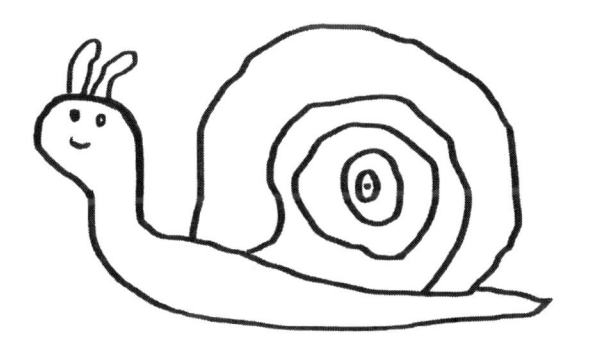

It's okay to take your time.

What do you need right now?

Your current needs are the most immediate roadmap to your well-being. Acknowledging them without judgment can not only bring relief but also guide your actions in a way that fosters your mental, emotional, and physical health.

What can you do today to take a step
towards healing and growth?

Personal growth and healing often start with small, deliberate steps. Posing this question forces you to sift through your emotional and psychological landscape to identify areas in need of attention. Whether it's reaching out for professional help, reconciling with past mistakes, or simply taking time for self-care, these little actions collectively make a strong significant impact.

If you had a friend who was feeling exactly the way you are right now, what would you say to them?

The advice you'd give to a friend in your situation is often the counsel you need yourself. This exercise of externalising your emotional state can offer valuable insights, as it's easier to offer empathy and wisdom to others than to ourselves.

Write down your self-care bucket list:

Creating a self-care bucket list is like drafting a love letter to yourself. Each item on the list is a commitment to your well-being, a pledge to listen to your body and soul. By actively noting what rejuvenates and enriches you, you're creating a reservoir of healing and peace, ready for the days when you'll need it the most.

What things would you like to do more,
and what's stopping you?

This is a question of priorities and obstacles. Desires to do 'more' of something, whether it's a hobby, spending time with loved ones, or pursuing a passion, are often indicative of what your soul yearns for. Identifying what's stopping you — be it time, resources, or fear — is like diagnosing the roadblocks on your path to fuller contentment.

What kind of people do you want
to surround yourself with?

The company you keep serves as a mirror reflecting your values, aspirations, and even your flaws. Aiming to surround yourself with certain types of people is, in essence, a form of self-selection, a way of curating your life experience and, by extension, your own personality and growth. Make a deliberate choice; choose companions who nourish your spirit, challenge your thinking, and fill your life with positivity.

What does your ideal day look like, from start to finish, and what's stopping you from making it happen?

Having an ideal day envisioned is the first step towards actualising it. From the activities that fill your time to the people who share these moments, your ideal day is a reflection of your innermost desires. Identifying what's stopping you is equally crucial; whether it's external obligations, internal fears, or logistical constraints, pinpointing these barriers can help you strategise ways to overcome them and make your ideal day a reality.

What drains your energy and makes you unhappy, and what things inspires and motivates you?

Your energy is your most valuable currency. Knowing what depletes it and what enriches it can empower you to make life choices that sustain your well-being and enthusiasm. This knowledge acts as a compass, guiding you towards experiences that invigorate your spirit and away from those that drain your vitality, fostering a life of balanced harmony and vibrant fulfillment.

Describe a moment when you felt a
deep sense of belonging:

Feeling a deep sense of belonging is one of the most affirming experiences we can have. It's a moment when the walls come down, when you feel deeply seen, valued, and secure. Whether it's a familial setting, a gathering of close friends, or even a personal milestone where everything just 'clicked,' these are the instances that resonate through your life, reminding you that you're not alone. Capturing this in words serves as a poignant reminder of your own worthiness of love and acceptance.

Write down your favourite quotes and
proverbs that you relate to:

Quotes and proverbs are like mental bookmarks, capturing wisdom and insights that resonate with your soul. By reflecting on them, you're creating a map of your inner universe, highlighting points of understanding that can guide you through life's complexities. This collection becomes a toolbox of inspiration, ready to help you through future challenges.

What habits do you wish to change? And what small steps can you take to make it happen?

Habits are the building blocks of daily life, and yet, they can either serve or impair you. Knowing which habits you wish to change implies that you're aware they're misaligned with your goals. The process of change often begins with this acknowledgment, leading to a journey that could entail struggle, self-reflection, and ultimately, transformation.

List the things that you would like to declutter
in your life to create a harmonious space:

Decluttering is not just about tidying up your physical space but also about clearing mental and emotional cobwebs. This cleansing process allows you to create a sanctuary, both within and without, conducive to clarity, peace, and joy. Identifying the clutter in your life, be it toxic relationships, unhealthy habits, or outdated beliefs, is the first step in a deeply healing journey toward balance and harmony.

How do you define success, and how close are you to achieving it?

Success is a deeply personal metric, influenced by societal norms, individual goals, and intrinsic values. Determining your own definition frees you from arbitrary benchmarks set by others and allows you to measure your life in ways that are meaningful to you. Knowing where you are in this journey towards your version of success helps you assess your path to make necessary adjustments.

How can you nurture your spirituality or
connect with your inner self?

Spirituality is a sanctuary for many, offering solace, clarity, and a sense of direction. This could involve religious practices, meditation, mindfulness, or even simple introspection in silence. Nurturing this facet of your life often brings emotional balance and a deeper understanding of yourself and the world around you.

What makes you happy beyond materialism?

The joy that resonates with the core of who you are often lies not in objects but in moments – in the quiet company of nature, the warm embrace of a family member, or the fulfillment that comes from a day spent in service to others. Delving into the depths of what brings you authentic happiness is not just an act of self-discovery; it's an expedition to the heart's true calling. It's in the shared smiles, the purpose-driven tasks, the gentle touch of kindness, and the vibrant threads of relationships that we experience a life rich with joy.

What small steps can you take today
to improve your life?

Improvement is a continuous journey, often achieved through incremental progress. Identifying those manageable steps is a practical way of turning lofty aspirations into achievable tasks. Whether it's adopting a healthier lifestyle, improving relationships, or advancing in your career, small actions can lay the foundation for significant transformations.

Write down a letter to God expressing how you feel?

In writing a letter to God, you may be seeking guidance during a confusing or difficult time. You can lay bare the fears and vulnerabilities that you've been reluctant to admit even to yourself. Your words could serve as a plea for understanding, asking for signs or answers that can help illuminate your path. This is an opportunity to be explicit about the questions that have been circling in your mind, and to openly ask for the wisdom to navigate life's complexities. It's a quest for a higher form of guidance that can bring you peace or clarity.

Create a gratitude list:

When we count our blessings, the world expands, and what seemed insignificant becomes a wellspring of joy. Gratitude turns what we have into enough, and more. It bridges the gap between lack and plenty, teaching us that true wealth is found in the richness of being and the depth of simple moments.

What positive affirmations can you use
to boost your confidence?

Positive affirmations act a little like emotional fuel, helping to shift your mindset and energise your confidence. Crafting these affirmations is like creating a personalised set of motivational slogans, designed to counter your self-doubts, elevate your self-esteem, and propel you forward.

Describe a moment when you felt truly alive and happy. How can you recreate a similar moment?

Moments of pure happiness and aliveness are emotional landmarks, serving as touchstones that can help reorient you when you're lost. The factors that converged to make such a moment possible, whether they were external circumstances, personal achievements, or a specific set of people, offer clues about what fundamentally satisfies your emotional and psychological needs. Understanding this allows you to intentionally seek and create more such moments.

Draw your happy place:

Sketching your 'happy place' is more than just an artistic endeavor; it's a blueprint for your ideal state of mind. This drawing represents your sanctuary, the space where you are most in tune with yourself. Even if you can't always physically be in that happy place, having a representation of it serves as a powerful mental anchor, a reminder of tranquility and joy amidst the storms of life.

How can you make a positive impact in the world?

Even as a single individual in a vast world, your capacity for positive impact is significant. Whether through your profession, your social influence, or your personal actions, identifying ways to contribute positively is an empowering exercise. It not only brings meaning and fulfilment but also connects you with others in a network of constructive change.

Your mind is a garden, what you feed it will grow.

NOTES

NOTES

NOTES

Reflections

As you close the pages of this journal, know that your journey inward is a courageous act of love for yourself and for those around you. The vulnerabilities you've embraced, the emotions you've navigated, the truths you've unearthed, and each line you've written is a step towards a more authentic, healed version of yourself.

While this journal may end, your path to self-understanding and healing doesn't. Take the insights you've gained and the clarity you've found as you forge ahead. May you continue to explore, heal, and grow, knowing that you carry within you an inexhaustible well of wisdom.

I CAN~~X~~ HEAL MYSELF

Healing isn't about repairing what's broken; it's about embracing all parts of you, even the cracks.

Mushin
Press

FREE MOOD JOURNAL

A simple tool to monitor and record your emotions and moods. To better understand yourself. To be more productive. To change your habits. It serves to identify triggers, mental health monitoring, goal tracking, mood patterns, positive reinforcement and self-awareness.

Scan QR code
to receive your free Mood Tracker Journal.

Printed in Great Britain
by Amazon

64d29f92-ee56-449b-815a-104883e350b0R02